How's Your Love Life?

Dennis Burke, Ph.D.

Printed in the United States of America. All rights reserved under International Copyright Law. Contents and/or cover may not be reproduced in whole or in part in any form without the expressed written consent of the Publisher.

Unless otherwise indicated, all Scripture quotations are taken from the *New King James Version* of the Bible.

How's Your Love Life?
ISBN 978-1-890026-07-3
© 1999 Dennis Burke

Dennis Burke Ministries
PO Box 150043
Arlington, TX 76015

The Amplified Bible © The Lockman Foundation, La Habra, California, 1954, 1958.

Good News Translation © 1992. American Bible Society, 1865 Broadway New York, NY.

New Living Translation © 1996. Tyndale House Publishers, Inc., Wheaton, Illinois.

The Message: The Bible in Contemporary Language © 2002. Eugene H. Peterson.

New Testament in Modern Speech © 1978. Kregel Publications, Grand Rapids, Michigan.

The Holy Bible, Revised Standard Version © 1952. William Collins Sons & Co., Ltd. New York, Glasgow & Toronto.

John G. Lake His Life, His Sermons, His Boldness of Faith © 1994. Kenneth Copeland Publications. Fort Worth, Texas.

Table of Contents

1 Believe the Love God Has for You .... Page 5

2 How's Your Love Life? ...... Page 21

3 Quest Worth Loving For ... Page 43

Chapter 1

Believe the Love God Has for You

There was something very different about the Apostle John. He was the youngest of all of Jesus' disciples, but a quality lay deep within John that set him apart from all the other disciples. You can see that difference at the Last Supper and again at the foot of the Cross as Jesus hung there agonizing. You can even see it after Jesus was raised from the dead.

In each of these instances, John is referred to as the disciple "whom Jesus loved." Even more revealing is the fact that John is referred to in this way in only one Gospel: the one he wrote himself. John described *himself* as "the one whom Jesus loved."

On the surface that could sound like arrogance, yet it actually points to something very powerful. It points to the revelation John had about himself —that Jesus loved him!

Throughout John's Gospel and the epistles he later wrote are found the Bible's deepest insights into God's love for you, as well as how to live in that divine love. John gives you more truth regarding God's love than any other writer of the New Testament. His insight originated in a deep, abiding knowledge of God's love for him personally.

Four times the Apostle John refers to himself as the disciple whom Jesus loved. John wasn't saying that he was the *only* disciple Jesus loved but that he *knew* he was loved by Jesus. It was a love John had come to believe in without reservation.

This God-kind of love is the Greek word *agape*—a unique word in the Greek text of the New Testament. *Agape* is a word that was nearly absent from Greek writing before the time of Jesus. It was only during Jesus' ministry that this word became a picture of God's love.

Of course, the God-kind of love is the highest love that exists. *Agape* knows no limits or boundaries as to how wide, deep, high, or far it will go to demonstrate love. *Agape* will sacrifice itself for the sake of the person so deeply loved. This love has no strings attached. It is not looking for what it can take from a relationship, but rather for what it can give. *Agape* so values the object loved that *nothing* will turn it away.

How's Your Love Life?

The message of the entire New Covenant centers around this simple fact: God's love for you is unconditional. This means you don't have to try to qualify for His love. You already qualify to receive it! You have no conditions to meet, and there is no pressure on you to measure up. Your Heavenly Father loves you just as you are, and there is nothing that can separate you from His love.

The Apostle Paul made this amazing statement about the God-kind of love:

> "For I am persuaded that neither death nor life, nor angels nor principali-

ties nor powers, nor things present nor things to come, nor height nor depth, nor any other created thing, shall be able to separate us from the love of God which is in Christ Jesus our Lord" (Romans 8:38-39).

Typically, the way people love one another is very different from God's love. Natural love is conditional. A person usually has to meet someone's expectations in order to be loved. Then later the recipient of natural love needs to requalify—and requalify again. In fact, in order to be loved by some people, a person needs to requalify almost daily!

The New Covenant has freed us from our own limited understanding of love and has revealed love on an entirely new level. Even the Old Testament was limited in its emphasis on love. The Law given to Moses focused on how people must love *God.* It pointed to people's obedience to God as the qualifier for receiving His love. On the other hand, the New Covenant provides the revelation of God's love for *us* — a love that has no limits.

You will never love God with all your heart until you have received His love for you.

First John 4:19 says, "We love Him because He first loved

How's Your Love Life?

us." Notice this verse from *The Message*: "We, though, are going to love—love and be loved. First we were loved, now we love. He loved us first."

The actual text leaves out the word *Him*. This difference is slight, yet the rich meaning deepens: We love because God first loved us. Our ability to love without requiring people to first qualify for our love comes only by receiving the love God has for us.

John, the Apostle of Love, sheds light on how we can grow up in our own walk with God by receiving His love.

"And we have known and believed the love that

God has for us. God is love, and he who abides in love abides in God, and God in him. Love has been perfected among us in this: that we may have boldness in the day of judgment; because as He is, so are we in this world. There is no fear in love; but perfect love casts out fear, because fear involves torment. But he who fears has not been made perfect in love. We love Him because He first loved us" (1 John 4:16-19).

Your choice to abide or to stay in God's love fills you with confidence, boldness, and a fearlessness that can come no

How's Your Love Life?

other way. You find a new depth of inner strength to face and to beat all opposition, because now you have the supernatural power that *agape* love generates. The power of the God-kind of love surges through you and flushes out fear. You need not fear failure, people, or disease. First, because *you* are loved, and, second, because you are empowered by His love.

Can you see yourself standing tall in the face of Satan's threats? You will when you believe there is nothing that will separate you from God's love and the resources of His Kingdom. And it is your Heavenly Father's good pleasure to give you His Kingdom (Luke 12:32).

How's Your Love Life?

Always remember—the focus of the New Testament is not on your love for God as much as it is on your coming to know the love He has for *you*. His love in you will drive out fear and every fear-fed issue in your life.

Consider the various things in life that are driven and fed by fear:

- Anger can be rooted in the fear that he won't get his way without intimidation.

- Procrastination is rooted in the fear of not doing something well.

- Shyness is based in a fear of people.

How's Your Love Life?

- The need to control people is rooted in fear and insecurity.

- Hoarding can be a fear of lack.

- Doubt originates in a person's fear that God's Word is not going to work for him.

These are some of the issues that will change when you receive a deep revelation regarding the truth *that you are one whom God loves*. Believing the love God has for you liberates you from the need to force your way through a situation. God can take care of the issues you have strained to control. He will flush out the destructive work fear has wrought in your soul to keep you tied up in your emotions. Then He will show you how to live freely from your heart—where His love reigns.

Looking back to where it all started in the Garden of Eden, you can see that as a result of sin, Adam's first response was to *fear*. God's answer to that fear was *love*, as manifested through the last Adam, Jesus. God's grace in sending His Son to redeem you is a revelation of His love. He has surrounded you with His love and grace, which has the power to overcome sin and all that sin has done to destroy mankind over the centuries.

How's Your Love Life?

Psalm 5:12 (*NLT*) says, "For you bless the godly, O Lord; you surround them with your shield of love." The *Good News Translation* says it this way: "You bless those who obey you, Lord; your love protects them like a shield."

When you believe the love God has for you, the shield is up and you are surrounded with love and protection. Declare it boldly: "You, Lord, have surrounded me with the shield of Your love!"

The Apostle John believed in the love God had for him. John died as an old man—the only original apostle of Jesus to live out his life. Whereas all the other eleven apostles of Jesus were martyred, John was exiled to a life of hard labor on the Isle of Patmos. There he wrote the Book of Revelation. Later he was released from Patmos and lived out his life in Ephesus. The Bishop of the Church of Ephesus in 190 AD writes of the Apostle John, who "fell asleep at Ephesus."

This great Apostle of Love found the simple and sustaining discovery of living life as "the disciple whom Jesus loved." You can discover the same life-changing truth. Determine to grow up in the knowledge of the God-kind of love. Allow your spiritual foundation to be built on the same truth this old apostle discovered back when he was a young disciple of the Messiah—that you, too, are a disciple whom Jesus loves.

Chapter 2

How Is Your Love Life?

You can tap into the deep, rich reservoir of God's love residing within you even when people rub you the wrong way. Love is a force much more powerful than human emotion.

The God-kind of love is the most powerful force in existence. It's even more powerful than any force known in the physical realm.

The Bible says God is love (1

John 4:8). This love has been imitated, misunderstood, and misrepresented. Yet God's love is the most powerful and important part of every true Christian's life. In fact, it's so important that if you are not growing in the God-kind of love, you are not really growing at all.

On the other hand, if you have made a life of love your goal, it makes every other aspect of life meaningful. Life becomes filled with the hope and the enjoyment God has always intended.

The God-kind of love touches every level of human existence: spirit, soul, and body. It is the most important ingredient in making your faith, prayer, or any other activity fulfilling—whether it's a natural or spiritual interest.

This kind of love is the foundation for the covenant God made with every Christian. The God-kind of love is beyond anything the natural mind could ever think or create. This new kind of love is born and developed in the recreated human spirit. <u>This love is one evidence that Jesus is alive in you.</u>

Knowledge alone has many limitations. Feelings and reasoning are undependable. But there are no limits in God's love which is totally reliable.

First Corinthians 8:1 says:

> "Mere knowledge causes people to be puffed up (to bear themselves loftily and be proud), but love (affection and goodwill and benevolence) edifies and builds up and encourages one to grow [to his full stature]" (*AMP*).

Love is God in Action

The word "agape" is the Greek word for the God-kind of love. Agape is God in action—His love demonstrated *through* the ones He loves, *toward* those who need His love.

Agape love denotes an overwhelming generosity and undefeateable goodwill that always seeks the highest good of the other person—no matter what he does. It is a self-giving love that gives freely without asking anything in return. It is a love based on choice and decision rather than feeling and emotion. Agape describes the unconditional love of God for every individual.

Love is a Decision

This God-kind of love acts quite different from natural, human love. For instance, to feel loved, some people tend to be performance-oriented. Others think they must do something to deserve love. That kind of love is purely human or natural love.

How's Your Love Life?

People who love with this natural type of love are governed by their emotions. Their love for others continually changes. Natural love is filled with conditions. This love says: "If you do something for me or give me the right thing, then I will continue to love you, otherwise you won't get my love."

In contrast, the believer who releases God's love chooses to love, then acts based on the decision he or she has made. Whether anyone responds or not, that believer has decided to be a person of love.

Any time we look at God's covenant love we must not forget to include First Corinthians 13:4-8:

"Love endures long and is patient and kind; love never is envious nor boils over with jealously, is not boastful or vainglorious, does not display itself haughtily. It is not conceited (arrogant and inflated with pride); it is not rude (unmannerly) and does not act unbecomingly.

"Love (God's love in us) does not insist on its own rights or its own way, for it is not self-seeking; it is not touchy or fretful or resentful; it takes no account of the evil done to it [it pays no attention to a suffered wrong].

How's Your Love Life?

"It does not rejoice at injustice and unrighteousness, but rejoices when right and truth prevail.

"Love bears up under anything and everything that comes, is ever ready to believe the best of every person, its hopes are fadeless under all circumstances, and it endures everything [with-out weakening]. Love never fails" (*AMP*).

How is your love life?

If you do not exhibit this God-kind of attitude in your life, then you must re-examine your commitment to walk in love. The qualities of God's love in this passage answer the question of what love truly looks like. In light of His love, reconsider your own love walk and let God's love grow in you.

Which Kind of Love?

In the Greek language there are four words that define love. The first is "agape" which is the God-kind of love. The second is "phileo" which is brotherly or friendly love. There is a sharp contrast between the two. One is born of the Spirit; the other is born of emotions. Where natural phileo love has its limits, agape is unlimited love. God's love born in your heart stands strong even in times when your emotions

How's Your Love Life?

have a reason to quit loving.

✻ Failed love that so many live with is rooted in the fear of giving themselves to others. They fear being ignored or rejected. Rather than becoming vulnerable with others, they interact with people in various ways. They may try to control, dominate, intimidate, or manipulate others.

If there are weak people around you like this, your love can overcome and compensate for their lack. You can see through their tactics and realize that the real issue is their insecurity in the presence of God and other people. You can rise up and overcome by walk-

How's Your Love Life?

ing in love that distinguishes us from ordinary people.

Proverbs 10:12 tells us that love does not get involved in strife. Instead, love conceals the weakness and sin of others. "Hatred stirs up strife, but love covers all sins."

Notice what Proverbs chapter 17 says about love:

"He who covers a transgression seeks love, but he who repeats a matter separates friends" (v. 9).

"A friend loves at all times..." (v. 17).

One of the most outstanding attributes of agape love is that

How's Your Love Life?

this love stands and does not fail or quit. Agape is one of the fruit of the spirit.

When the Squeeze is on, What Comes Out?

The following questions will help you determine whether or not God's love is working in you. When you are squeezed by problems or people what comes out? Is it the love of God or anger and fear? Are you intolerant of people? How do you *display* your love?

Everyone gets rubbed the wrong way by people, but not everyone draws on the love of God that is deposited within them for such occasions. Too often, excuses are used to justify rude or angry reactions. Only after you become honest with yourself can you fully grasp the way others already see you.

Are you patient and kind as the Bible describes love? Or do you bark and bite at people like a junkyard dog, all the while justifying yourself as you do?

It is easy to justify nearly any action. You can let your anger and temper flare with a sense of total justification using worn out excuses like, "They don't know the troubles I have had" or "Why can't they just do what I say?"

A Reason, But No Excuse

There can be countless reasons for letting out your hostility, but there is no real excuse. Love refuses to allow anger to dominate. Proverbs 12:16 tells us, "A fool's wrath is known at once, but a prudent man covers shame."

God's love in you is patient and kind. Kindness is a very underdeveloped aspect of the fruit of the Spirit. Kindness demonstrates the lordship of Jesus in your life. The Holy Spirit will supply the necessary strength to change every deep-rooted weakness in your life.

The way you handle people demonstrates the depth of your

understanding of God's Word. First John 4:8 says, "He who does not love does not know God, for God is love." Verse 20 further emphasizes this truth:

> "If someone says, 'I love God,' and hates his brother, he is a liar, for he who does not love his brother whom he has seen, how can he love God whom he has not seen?"

Simple Social Skills

The Amplified Bible says the God-kind of love is not rude but mannerly. Simple social skills, such as manners, do not make you fake or insincere. Instead they give you the tools to express in verbal and non-verbal ways that you genuinely value people.

For example, to make eye contact with a person and listen when he is speaking to you expresses your interest and attention. You really listen with your eyes as much as your ears. In a non-verbal way, you are placing value on a person, and they will recognize it and feel appreciated.

We are always supposed to be honest, but honesty isn't an excuse for being rude. You may justify yourself by saying, "But that is just the way I am." Then let the Holy Spirit help you become more like Jesus.

Moodiness is another excuse

How's Your Love Life?

for not acting in love. Moody people are double-minded people. They cannot be relied upon because no one knows if they will be in the mood to do what is needed.

Moody people may believe in God's love, but excuse their poor treatment of others to their mood. Moodiness is an unwillingness to take the higher road to walk in love by faith instead of reacting emotionally. Faith will not only overcome the world but also the emotions that have ruled your life.

Give It Away

How do you *distribute* your love? Jesus indicated you distribute the God-kind of love by giving away your greatest riches.

One of the greatest examples of this love is found in the story of the good Samaritan. When Jesus gave this example, He was responding to a question from an insincere lawyer regarding what he must do to inherit eternal life. First Jesus asked what he thought, then confirmed his right answer:

> "You shall love the Lord your God with all your heart, with all you soul, with all your strength, and with all your mind, and your neighbor as yourself" (Luke 10:27).

Jesus responded to this insincere lawyer by saying, "You have answered rightly; do this and you will live" (verse 28).

Here is a man who knew the right answer but was not living according to what he knew. Jesus then told the story of a man who was a Samaritan—a half-breed who was unacceptable to the people of Israel.

There was a man on the road to Jericho who had been beaten by thieves and left half dead. A priest and a Levite both came by but did nothing to help this man. Then the Samaritan came and "had compassion" on him.

"So he went to him and bandaged his wounds,

pouring on oil and wine; and he set him on his own animal, brought him to an inn, and took care of him.

"On the next day, when he departed, he took out two denarii, gave them to the innkeeper, and said to him, 'Take care of him; and whatever more you spend, when I come again, I will repay you.'

"So which of these three do you think was neighbor to him who fell among the thieves? And he said, 'He who showed mercy on him.'

"Then Jesus said to him,

'Go and do likewise'" (vv. 34-37).

This man heard about love in action. Love bandaged the man where he hurt and took him to a place of safety. Love cared for him, and paid to do it. Love acted without needing to be repaid. Love will do more than seems reasonable and do it with joy.

The Samaritan knew that his money was not to be used only on himself, but also to help someone in need. Thank God he was prosperous or we would not have this story.

The God-kind of love is deposited in your heart, or your

inner man. In Romans 5:5 it says:

"Now hope does not disappoint, because the love of God has been poured out in our hearts by the Holy Spirit who was given to us."

You are to give from a heart of love because God gave, not because someone deserves it. The heart of love doesn't look to do as little as possible, but rather it goes as far as it can to express God's great love.

Chapter 3

Quest Worth Loving For

What motivates your decisions? Do you react in an effort to protect yourself from the hurts and actions of others—whether they be remembered or anticipated? Do you respond to the circumstances that come against you from the outside? Or does God's gift of unconditional love burn within the very core of your being?

You were not made for hate or fear. You were made for a

life of love. The challenge you face is that the natural course of life is spiraling downward and away from the loving attitudes that the Word of God describes for your life.

Pursue Love

Some people can be hard, manipulative, and self-serving. Even among Christians, it is not common to find those who let love dominate their lives. But there is a way to reverse the downward spiral we face. Paul says to simply, "Pursue love" (1 Corinthians 14:1).

This passage is not talking about pursuing the natural, worldly kind of love. Natural love only does well in an atmosphere of appreciation and friendship. It grows when there is mutual affection and respect. However, if this natural love is not returned, it can quickly grow cold or even become harsh and bitter.

Natural love may begin with deep feelings that would appear to last forever. Yet, many times marriage starts with the commitment "until death do us part" and turns into a painfully cold, unfulfilling relationship.

The good news is that there is a different kind of love available to Christians. Romans 5:5 says, "God's love for us floods our hearts through the Holy Spirit" (*Weymouth*). After you are born again, love takes you over and washes through the center of your being.

God's Love is Perfect

The God-kind of love is perfect love. It is without question the greatest of all the fruit of the Spirit dwelling within the believer. Nothing is more necessary in the life of a believer than love, and nothing makes life richer. Every believer must make love a lifelong quest.

The strength of the God-kind of love will keep you stable and free from the fluctuating feelings that pull many people down. Love will free you to honor others even when they have disappointed you.

How's Your Love Life?

When you are born again, you are a carrier and container of God's love. The world needs to experience the God-kind of love flowing from you.

You have been recreated to be an expression of God's love —a light of hope to the masses who are dark and depressed.

No matter how they may act, people who have never experienced God's love do not need harshness or condemnation. They need the message of the gospel that love is not earned but received freely through a relationship with Jesus Christ.

The love of God that resides

in your heart is one of the most powerful aspects of the new birth. The strength of this love does not depend on other people's actions. It will even move you into positive action toward those who despitefully use you. Jesus not only commands you to love, but also He fully supplies the grace to do it.

A Gift to Develop

God's love in you is a gift, but it must be developed before it will help you deal with the pressures you face in every day life. God's love doesn't increase in you by merely trying harder or holding your negative feelings inside. Instead, love grows as a result of entering His presence.

How's Your Love Life?

The key to developing the God-kind of love is learning to shift from living under the rule of your emotions and reactions to living from the inner man where love dwells.

As a believer, you are no longer free to respond to people based on your feelings or emotions. Instead, you must choose to act according to the new law of God that has been born anew within your heart— a law James 2:8 calls the royal law of love.

Put on Love

Love must be put on in the same way you dress yourself at the beginning of the day. Before you meet the day, you must choose to put on love—

How's Your Love Life?

God's love within—draped over you from the inside out. It will greet everyone you meet, and it will speak with greater impact than words alone.

Notice what Colossians says about putting on love:

> "Therefore, as the elect of God, holy and beloved, put on tender mercies, kindness, humility, meekness, longsuffering; bearing with one another, and forgiving one another, if anyone has a complaint against another; even as Christ forgave you, so you also must do. But above all of these things put on love, which is the bond of

perfection" (Colossians 3: 12-14).

Love Determines Maturity

The term "the bond of perfection" means that love ties you to maturity. Only to the degree that you choose to practice the God-kind of love in your life will you grow in all aspects of Christian living.

Without this God-kind of love gaining prominence, you will find that your effectiveness and strength are not what they should be. Again First Corinthians 13, the love chapter, reveals just how shallow spiritual activity really is without God's love as the foundation:

"Though I speak with the tongues of men and of angels, but have not love, I have become sounding brass or a clanging cymbal."

"And though I have the gift of prophecy, and understand all mysteries and all knowledge, and though I have all faith, so that I could remove mountains, but have not love, I am nothing.

"And though I bestow all my goods to feed the poor, and though I give my body to be burned, but have not love, it profits me nothing" (verses 1-3).

How's Your Love Life?

Notice that prayer does not bring effective results if your love life is amiss. What about prophecy, teaching, or exercising faith? None of it is of any value if love is not your motive for living. If it is without love, even giving money or deep personal sacrifice will not bring any increase as it should.

Love is the Foundation

Love is the foundational motive of all that God has deemed spiritual and holy. Without love as the central governing force, all other spiritual endeavors produce little and remain very shallow.

This point is made quite

forcefully by John G. Lake, a man whose healing ministry early in the 20th century was one of the greatest this nation has seen. In his book, *John G. Lake Sermons*, he noted one of the problems he had seen with the various moves of God in his day: "We were absorbed in the phenomena of God, not in God Himself. Now we must go on!"

Every move of God and all manifestations of God are wonderful, but you must be focused on the reason for it all—to lift people out of the works of the devil and show them the love that God has for them.

Lake went on to tell what he saw for the future:

"I can see as my spirit discerns the future and reaches out to touch the heart of mankind and the desire of God, that there is coming from heaven a new manifestation of the Holy Ghost in power, and that new manifestation will be in sweetness, in love, in tenderness, in the power of the Spirit, beyond anything your heart, or mind ever saw. The very lightning of God will flash through men's souls. The sons of God will meet the sons of darkness and prevail."

In the 20th century, Lake saw something about the days we are living in today. These are the days when the Holy Spirit is moving in overwhelming power. But it is also the increase of love and sweet tenderness in the Holy Spirit's power that will demonstrate to the world the depth of God that is beyond mere words.

> If you are going to focus on God's power, you must keep His love, gentleness, and kindness at the center of everything you do and say.

Covenant Love

Jonathan, David's covenant friend, was killed in battle along with his father King Saul. Years later, when David became king in Israel, he searched his entire kingdom to find a descendent of his covenant friend. David was overcome with the desire to show kindness—his covenant love for Jonathan—and he would not rest until a descendent of Jonathan was found.

Love must become your motive for the miracles, kindness, giving, and all your other activities. Paul said it this way, "For the love of Christ controls us" (2 Corinthians 5:14 *RSV*). Love is always to be the dominant force in your life.

Love is so important that according to Ephesians 3:19 the fullness of God is directly linked to knowing the love of Christ:

> "To know the love of Christ which passes

knowledge; that you may be filled with all the fullness of God."

When you develop a greater understanding of God's love within you, and experience that love demonstrated through you, He will fulfill your life in ways you have never dreamed possible.

This life of love is the best way to live. It will give you the strength and control that Jesus demonstrated in His life. It enables you to rule over your emotions and remain unmoved by the actions and words of others. It makes you gentle and Christ-like in the midst of difficulties. It makes your walk, your talk, your actions, and your reactions a testimony to the goodness and power of God that dwells in your heart.

Make a fresh decision to pursue the God-kind of love in your life today!

Dennis Burke is internationally known as a Bible teacher and best-selling author. He has helped thousands of people discover victorious living through faith in God's Word.

Dennis began in ministry as an associate pastor in California, then moved to Texas to work with Kenneth Copeland Ministries. His involvement with Kenneth Copeland Ministries continues as a guest speaker and contributing author for the *Believers' Voice of Victory* magazine.

Dennis serves as president for an international ministers organization (ICFM) and has been the keynote speaker in retreats, conventions, seminars and churches.

Books by Dr. Dennis Burke

*Dreams Really Do Come True —
It Can Happen to You!*

Develop A Winning Attitude

Breaking Financial Barriers

You Can Conquer Life's Conflicts

Grace: Power Beyond Your Ability

* How to Meditate God's Word

Knowing God Intimately

*A Guide to Successfully Attaining
Your God-given Goals*

The Law of the Wise

* Available in Spanish

CDs by Dr. Dennis Burke

Creating an Atmosphere and Attitude for Increase

The Transfer of Wealth

The Tithe – Your Blessing Connection

Learning to Yield to the Holy Spirit

How to Cast Off Whatever Has Cast You Down

How to Bring Your Dreams to Life

Secrets to Developing Strength of Character

Books by Vikki Burke

Aim Your Child Like An Arrow

Relief From Stress

Breaking Free From Guilt, Shame and Blame

Divine Protection for Dangerous Days

The Power of Peace — Protection and Direction

CDs by Vikki Burke

Too Blessed to Be Stressed

Pressing Through the Promise into Possession

Burn with Passion — Reach a Higher Level of Living

For a complete list of books,
audio and video messages by
Dennis and Vikki Burke,
or to receive the free publication,
Insights, A Way to New Life

Visit their website at:
www.dennisburkeministries.org

Or write:

Dennis Burke Ministries
PO Box 150043
Arlington, TX 76015
(817) 277-9627

Include your prayer requests.